Contents

How to be a times tables detective!

Times tables are full of patterns and connections. If you know these, it will help you to remember the times tables. It will also help you to use the tables to solve problems and to reason about numbers. There are detectives in this book who will help you to spot patterns. They will also sometimes ask a question to challenge you. When you spot a detective, take the chance to think in a bit more depth, and become a times tables detective!

Colour the multiples of 6.

 Count along 6 to mark the numbers in the ×6 table.

1	2	3	4	5	6	7	8	9	10
11	12	13	14	15	16	17	18	19	20
21	22	23	24	25	26	27	28	29	30
31	32	33	34	35	36	37	38	39	40
41	42	43	44	45	46	47	48	49	50
51	52	53	54	55	56	57	58	59	60

 Count in 6s on the number line and write in each multiple of 6.

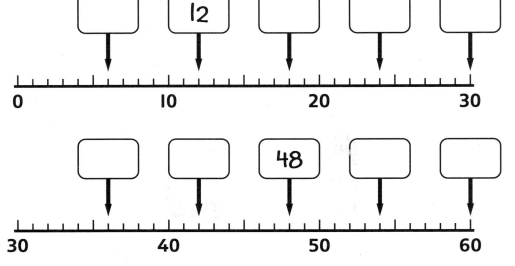

What will the next two numbers in the sequence be? _____

6	12		24	

_____

		48	54	

_____

66		78		90

_____

_____

Write the missing numbers from the ×6 table. Explain how the three grids are connected. Use these words: tens, ones.

4

Double 3s

T What numbers go into and come out of the function machine?

Work out the ×3 multiplication, then double it.

$4 \times 3 =$ | 12 | ┄┄→   ┄┄→ | 24 |

$6 \times 3 =$ | | ──→

$3 \times 3 =$ | | ┄┄→

$7 \times 3 =$ | | ──→

$9 \times 3 =$ | | ┄┄→

double

S Complete the multiplication grid.

×	3	5	10	2	7	6	11	4	8	12	9
3	9										
6	18										

D Complete the calculations to find the numbers that go into the function machine.

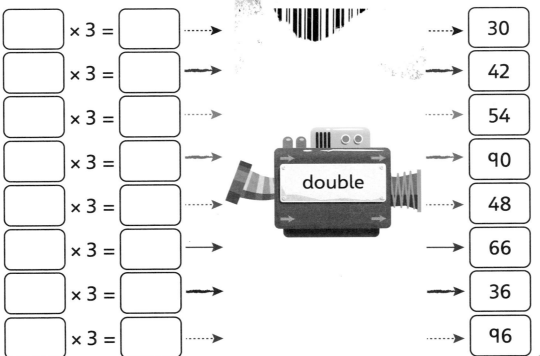

	× 3 =		┄┄→ ┄┄→	30
	× 3 =		──→ ──→	42
	× 3 =		┄┄→ ┄┄→	54
	× 3 =		──→ ──→	90
	× 3 =		┄┄→ ┄┄→	48
	× 3 =		──→ ──→	66
	× 3 =		──→ ──→	36
	× 3 =		┄┄→ ┄┄→	96

double

What do you have to do to the output to get back to the starting number?

How much money is in each group?   = 5p   = 1p

1  12 p

2 p

3  p

4   p

5     p

 Complete a number sentence for each of the amounts above.

1 ⬚ × 6 = ⬚   **2** ⬚ × 6 = ⬚

3 ⬚ × 6 = ⬚   **4** ⬚ × 6 = ⬚

5 ⬚ × 6 = ⬚

Explain how to use the ×5 table to work out the ×6 table.

_____

_____

 For every 1p coin, there is a 5p coin. How many coins are there altogether in each amount?

Is there a quick way to find each answer?

24p ⬚	42p ⬚	54p ⬚	
36p ⬚	60p ⬚	48p ⬚	
72p ⬚	30p ⬚	66p ⬚	
90p ⬚	£1·80 ⬚	£6·06 ⬚	

Triangles of 6

×6

 T How many counters are there in each group of triangles?

  12

Each triangle has 6 counters. Multiply the number of triangles by 6.

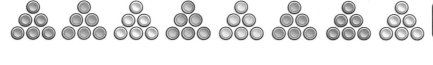

 S Write the answer to each ×6 calculation.
Match each calculation to the correct group of triangles.

3 × 6 = [ ]

7 × 6 = [ ]

5 × 6 = [ ]

8 × 6 = [ ]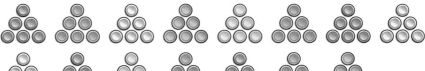

6 × 6 = [ ]

 D Tom counted groups of counters. How many triangles of 6 counters can he make for each group?

18 counters [ ]   30 counters [ ]   24 counters [ ]

42 counters [ ]   37 counters [ ]   47 counters [ ]

Which have some counters left over? How many counters?

_____

7

Use ×6 table facts to find the number of eggs in each question.

$\boxed{3} \times \boxed{6} = \boxed{18}$

$\boxed{} \times \boxed{} = \boxed{}$

$\boxed{} \times \boxed{} = \boxed{}$

$\boxed{} \times \boxed{} = \boxed{}$

$\boxed{} \times \boxed{} = \boxed{}$

 An egg box contains 6 eggs. How many egg boxes are needed for each group of eggs? Write the division for each question.

$\boxed{} \div \boxed{} = \boxed{}$

$\boxed{} \div \boxed{} = \boxed{}$

$\boxed{} \div \boxed{} = \boxed{}$

$\boxed{} \div \boxed{} = \boxed{}$

$\boxed{} \div \boxed{} = \boxed{}$

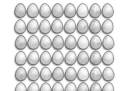

$\boxed{} \div \boxed{} = \boxed{}$

 Circle the numbers of eggs that will fit exactly into boxes of 6.

48   36   16   24   56   42   18   62   72   30   44   54

Take one lot away

 T Write how many white squares are in each array.

1 ⬜⬜⬜⬜⬜⬜⬜⬜⬜▪ **18**

2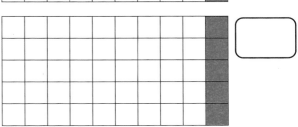

3 ⬜⬜⬜⬜⬜⬜⬜⬜▪ ⬜

4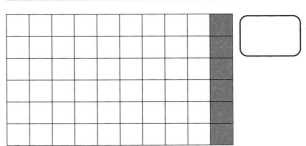

5 ⬜⬜⬜⬜⬜⬜⬜⬜▪ ⬜

6 ⬜

S Write number sentences for each of the arrays above.

1 [2] × 10 = [20] − [2] = [18]

2 [ ] × 10 = [ ] − [ ] = [ ]

3 [ ] × 10 = [ ] − [ ] = [ ]

4 [ ] × 10 = [ ] − [ ] = [ ]

5 [ ] × 10 = [ ] − [ ] = [ ]

6 [ ] × 10 = [ ] − [ ] = [ ]

D Write each calculation as a ×9 multiplication.

30 − 3 = [3] × 9 = [27]   40 − 4 = [ ] × 9 = [ ]

60 − 6 = [ ] × 9 = [ ]   90 − 9 = [ ] × 9 = [ ]

50 − 5 = [ ] × 9 = [ ]   20 − 2 = [ ] × 9 = [ ]

70 − 7 = [ ] × 9 = [ ]   80 − 8 = [ ] × 9 = [ ]

 100 − 10 = [ ] × 9 = [ ]

T Write the answers to the multiplications.
Use the bar chart to check your answers.

3 × 10 = [ ]   4 × 9 = [ ]

6 × 10 = [ ]   5 × 9 = [ ]

8 × 10 = [ ]   3 × 9 = [ ]

7 × 10 = [ ]   7 × 9 = [ ]

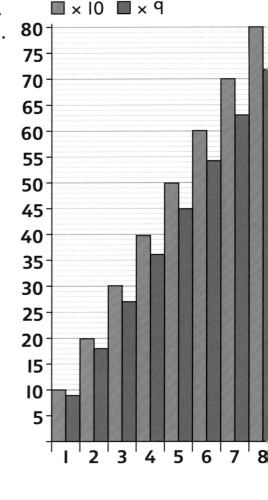

■ × 10   ■ × 9

 S Use the bar chart to find the difference
between the ×9 and ×10 tables.

three 10s – three 9s = [ ]

five 10s – five 9s = [ ]

seven 10s – seven 9s = [ ]

four 10s – four 9s = [ ]

eight 10s – eight 9s = [ ]

six 10s – six 9s = [ ]

 What do you
notice about
each answer?

 D Add together bars on the chart to find the answers.
Or multiply by 10 instead of 9 and subtract the multiplier.

14 × 9 = [ ]   15 × 9 = [ ]

18 × 9 = [ ]   13 × 9 = [ ]

21 × 9 = [ ]   27 × 9 = [ ]

For 14 × 9 you could add
the bars for 6 × 9 and
8 × 9 because 6 + 8 = 14.

Linking to 3s

A small box contains 3 chocolates.
A large box contains 3 small boxes (9 chocolates).

  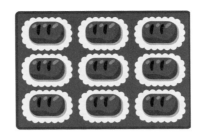

I chocolate   I small box   I large box

 Complete the table to show the number of small boxes and the number of chocolates in each large box.

Large boxes	1	2	3	4	5	6
Small boxes	3					
Chocolates	9					

 How many chocolates are in the boxes?

4 small boxes   [4] × [3] = [12]

2 large boxes   [ ] × [9] = [ ]

7 large boxes   [ ] × [ ] = [ ]

6 large boxes   [ ] × [ ] = [ ]

7 small boxes   [ ] × [ ] = [ ]

 Join together multiplications that have the same product.

| 9 × 3 | 27 × 3 | 18 × 3 | 12 × 3 | 6 × 3 | 30 × 3 | 21 × 3 |

| 4 × 9 | 3 × 9 | 10 × 9 | 6 × 9 | 9 × 9 | 2 × 9 | 7 × 9 |

Digit sums

 Write the digit sum for each multiple of 9.

Can you see a pattern?

1st multiple = | 9 | 0 + 9 = 9

2nd multiple = | 18 | 1 + 8 = 9

3rd multiple = | | | | + | | = | |

4th multiple = | | | | + | | = | |

5th multiple = | | | | + | | = | |

6th multiple = | | | | + | | = | |

7th multiple = | | | | + | | = | |

8th multiple = | | | | + | | = | |

 Complete the digit sums of some larger multiples of 9.

9th multiple = | | | | + | | = | |

10th multiple = | | | | + | | = | |

11th multiple = | | | | + | | = | |

               | | + | | = | |

12th multiple = | | | | + | | + | | = | |

 Write the missing digit each time to make a 3-digit multiple of 9.

2 ☐ 6   4 ☐ 8   53 ☐   34 ☐

5 ☐ 7   9 ☐ 5   77 ☐   6 ☐ 5

Pattern in 9s

 Write the ×9 fact for each row.

1	2	3	4	5	6	7	8	9
10	11	12	13	14	15	16	17	18
19	20	21	22	23	24	25	26	27
28	29	30	31	32	33	34	35	36
37	38	39	40	41	42	43	44	45

$1 \times 9 = 9$

$2 \times 9 = \boxed{}$

$3 \times \boxed{} = \boxed{}$

$\boxed{} \times \boxed{} = \boxed{}$

$\boxed{} \times \boxed{} = \boxed{}$

 Here is part of a 100 square. Write in the multiples of 9.

31					36				

Describe the pattern you see. _____

_____

 Write the multiples of 9 from 9 to 108. Explain the patterns that you notice. Use these words: tens, ones, increases, decreases.

_____

_____

_____

5s, 2s and 7s

 T Calculate the number of white squares and the number of yellow squares in each array.

1
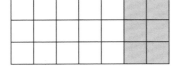

3 × 5 = 15

3 × 2 = 6

2
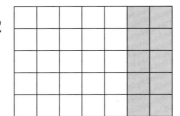

☐ × 5 = ☐

☐ × 2 = ☐

3
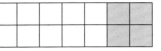

☐ × 5 = ☐

☐ × 2 = ☐

4
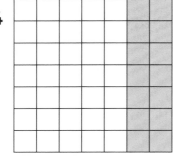

☐ × 5 = ☐

☐ × 2 = ☐

5
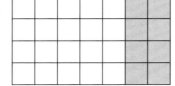

☐ × 5 = ☐

☐ × 2 = ☐

6
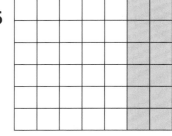

☐ × 5 = ☐

☐ × 2 = ☐

 S For each of the arrays above, complete the multiplication.

1 ☐ × 7 = ☐   **2** ☐ × 7 = ☐

3 ☐ × 7 = ☐   **4** ☐ × 7 = ☐

5 ☐ × 7 = ☐   **6** ☐ × 7 = ☐

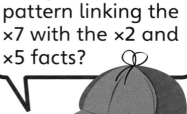
Can you spot a pattern linking the ×7 with the ×2 and ×5 facts?

 D Complete the divisions.

☐ ÷ 7 = 6   ☐ ÷ 7 = 2   ☐ ÷ 7 = 4

☐ ÷ 7 = 7   ☐ ÷ 7 = 9   ☐ ÷ 7 = 5

☐ ÷ 7 = 3   ☐ ÷ 7 = 12   ☐ ÷ 7 = 8

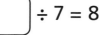

Zigzag 7s

T Each part of the zigzag is 7 cm long. What is the total length of the zigzag from Start to each of the points marked?

Use the ×7 table to help you.

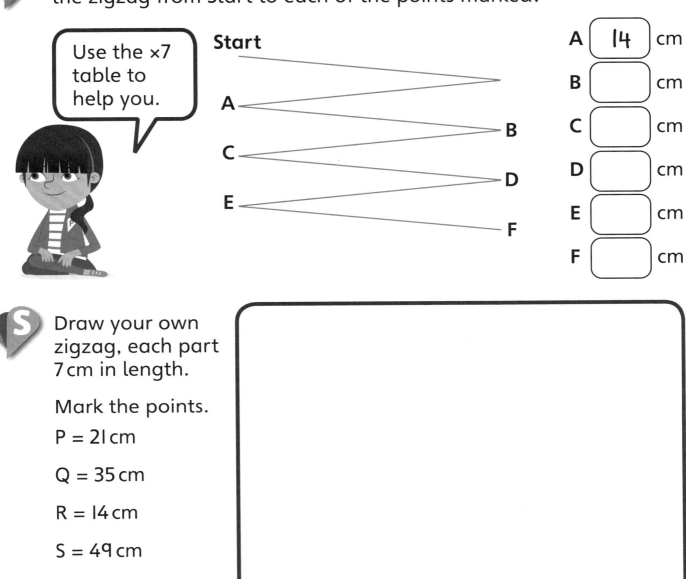

A	14	cm
B		cm
C		cm
D		cm
E		cm
F		cm

S Draw your own zigzag, each part 7 cm in length.

Mark the points.

P = 21 cm

Q = 35 cm

R = 14 cm

S = 49 cm

T = 28 cm

D Zigzag lines are drawn with total lengths shown. How many 7 cm lines make each line?

35 cm ☐   56 cm ☐   70 cm ☐

42 cm ☐   63 cm ☐   28 cm ☐

84 cm ☐   49 cm ☐   140 cm ☐

T A number line is made from rods. A rod is worth 7.
Fill in the missing numbers.

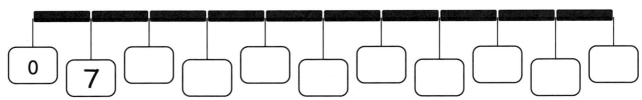

| 0 | 7 | | | | | | | | |

S A rod is worth 7. Write the multiplication and calculate the number represented by each group of rods.

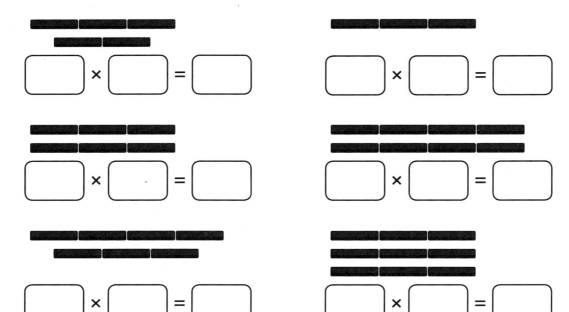

◯ × ◯ = ◯   ◯ × ◯ = ◯

◯ × ◯ = ◯   ◯ × ◯ = ◯

◯ × ◯ = ◯   ◯ × ◯ = ◯

D A rod is worth 7. How many whole rods do you need to represent each number?

35 ☐   49 ☐   84 ☐   45 ☐   73 ☐

56 ☐   28 ☐   63 ☐   59 ☐   80 ☐

Four numbers above have a remainder. Which numbers? What is the remainder?

Numbers _____

Remainder _____

16

Match to add

 T Join each multiplication to an addition with the same answer.

(4 × 7) (2 × 7) (5 × 7) (6 × 7) (3 × 7) (10 × 7)

(10 + 11) (20 + 15) (20 + 22) (10 + 4) (40 + 30) (20 + 8)

 S Write the missing numbers.

> First work out the side with no missing number.

5 × 7 = 30 + ☐   3 × 7 = ☐ + 6

☐ × 7 = 35 + 7   ☐ × 7 = 14 + 14

☐ × 7 = 25 + 24   8 × 7 = 36 + ☐

☐ × 7 = 35 + 35   9 × 7 = 45 + ☐

 D Use the four numbers in each set to make calculations that have the same answer. One side must be multiplication or division by 7 and the other must be addition or subtraction.

Write +, −, × and ÷ signs in the circles.

7, 21, 25, 28   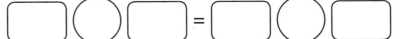 ☐ ◯ ☐ = ☐ ◯ ☐

5, 7, 15, 20   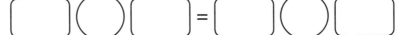 ☐ ◯ ☐ = ☐ ◯ ☐

3, 5, 7, 56   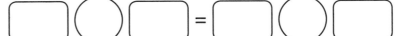 ☐ ◯ ☐ = ☐ ◯ ☐

6, 7, 18, 60   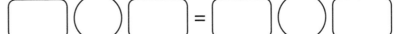 ☐ ◯ ☐ = ☐ ◯ ☐

7, 9, 21, 42   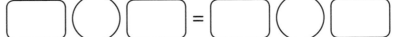 ☐ ◯ ☐ = ☐ ◯ ☐

7, 33, 45, 84   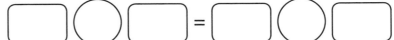 ☐ ◯ ☐ = ☐ ◯ ☐

×7

Class 4 have been asked to make cuddly aliens. Each alien must have 7 button eyes and 4 arms.

T How many buttons are needed to make the number of aliens shown?

Use the ×7 table.

4 aliens [28] buttons   6 aliens [ ] buttons

3 aliens [ ] buttons   10 aliens [ ] buttons

9 aliens [ ] buttons   5 aliens [ ] buttons

S How many aliens can you make with the number of buttons shown?

35 buttons [ ] aliens   14 buttons [ ] aliens

49 buttons [ ] aliens   28 buttons [ ] aliens

63 buttons [ ] aliens   84 buttons [ ] aliens

D Buttons come in packs of 6. How many buttons are left over if you make the numbers of aliens below?

3 aliens, 4 packs [ ]   5 aliens, 6 packs [ ]

4 aliens, 5 packs [ ]   6 aliens, 7 packs [ ]

How many packs of buttons would you need for 8 aliens? [ ]

How many buttons are there?
How many buttons will you use?

How much money is in each group?   = 5p   = 1p

  22p

     p

    p

    p

    p

 Use equal numbers of 10p coins and 1p coins to make each of these amounts.

44p = [4] 10p and [4] 1p   66p = [   ] 10p and [   ] 1p

33p = [   ] 10p and [   ] 1p   77p = [   ] 10p and [   ] 1p

55p = [   ] 10p and [   ] 1p   99p = [   ] 10p and [   ] 1p

 Starting in January, Sameer saves £11 every month. What month will it be when he has saved the following amounts?

£55 _____   £77 _____

£99 _____   £44 _____

£66 _____   £33 _____

£132 _____   £220 _____

How much money will he have saved after 2 years? £ [   ]

Complete the table to make ×11 facts.

Check that the ×1 row and ×10 row add to make the ×11 row.

×	2	3	4	5	6	7	8	9
1	2							
10	20							
11	22							

 In this table, the numbers 2 to 9 go in the top row, but not in order. Fill in all the missing numbers.

×		9					8	
1				5	4			
10	30		60				70	
11								

How do you find the numbers missing from the top row?

 In this table, the numbers 12 to 22 go in the top row, but not in order. Fill in all the missing numbers.

×				19		16			18		
10		140					220			170	130
11	165		231		220			132			

Jasmine and Luc are playing a game using the multiples of 11.
Circle the numbers they can use.

48　(88)　27　134　71　44　86　51

11　74　45　110　31　22　100　111　33　16

122　32　77　13　53　66　56　30　99　121

Which 2-digit multiple of 11 is not shown? [　　]

 Write each multiple of 11 above as a ×11 calculation.

[8] × 11 = [88]　　[　] × 11 = [　]

[　] × 11 = [　]　　[　] × 11 = [　]

[　] × 11 = [　]　　[　] × 11 = [　]

[　] × 11 = [　]　　[　] × 11 = [　]

[　] × 11 = [　]　　[　] × 11 = [　]

[　] × 11 = [　]

What pattern do you spot?

 Complete each calculation so it is correct.

4 × 11 = [44] + [4] = 48　　66 ÷ 11 = [　] + [　] = 27

99 ÷ 11 = [　] + [　] = 33　　7 × 11 = [　] − 43 = [　]

[　] ÷ 6 = 88 ÷ 11　　12 × 11 = 200 − [　]

How much money is in each amount? = £2  = £10

£ 36   £ ___   £ ___

£ ___   £ ___   £ ___

Sam earns £12 as a £10 note and a £2 coin each week. Write how much he will earn after:

2 weeks	£	4 weeks	£	5 weeks	£
8 weeks	£	10 weeks	£	7 weeks	£
6 weeks	£	9 weeks	£	12 weeks	£

Kiya has a £2 coin for every £10 note. If she has the amount shown in £10 notes, how much money does she have altogether?

£30	£	£60	£	£100	£
£50	£	£80	£	£90	£
£110	£	£70	£	£120	£

Link to 3s and 4s

T Circle the multiples of 3 and draw a triangle around the multiples of 4.

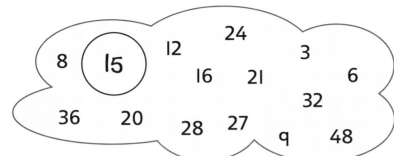

8 15 12 24 3
16 21 6
32
36 20 28 27 9 48

What do you notice about the numbers that have a circle and a triangle around them?

Write the numbers that are multiples of 3 **and** 4.

_____

S Join calculations with the same product. One calculation does not have a match. Write a calculation to match it.

9 × 4	8 × 3	4 × 3	6 × 4	20 × 3	8 × 2 × 3	

3 × 12	1 × 12	2 × 12	4 × 12	7 × 12	5 × 12

D Tick all the calculations whose product is also a multiple of 12.

9 × 3 = ☐ ☐   7 × 4 = ☐ ☐   8 × 3 = ☐ ☐

9 × 4 = ☐ ☐   10 × 4 = ☐ ☐   16 × 3 = ☐ ☐

15 × 4 = ☐ ☐   14 × 3 = ☐ ☐   11 × 4 = ☐ ☐

13 × 3 = ☐ ☐   21 × 4 = ☐ ☐   24 × 3 = ☐ ☐

What do you notice about ×3 or ×4 multiplications that result in a multiple of 12?

Double 6

 T What numbers come out of the function machine?

4 × 6 = 24 → → 48

6 × 6 = ☐ ·····► ·····► ☐

3 × 6 = ☐ → → ☐

7 × 6 = ☐ → → ☐

9 × 6 = ☐ ► ► ☐

5 × 6 = ☐ ·····► ·····► ☐

8 × 6 = ☐ → → ☐

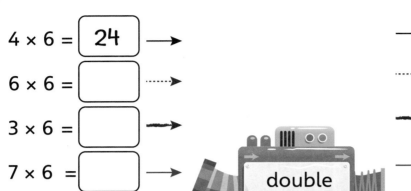 double

 Work out the × multiplication first, then doub[le]

S Complete the multiplication grid.

×	3			7	11		8		9
6		30		12					
12			120		72	48		144	

D Numbers are multiplied by 6 and the answer is doubled.
Fill in the missing numbers.

☐ × 6 → → 36
☐ × 6 ·····► ·····► 48
☐ × 6 → double → → 108
☐ × 6 ·····► ·····► 84
☐ × 6 → → 144
☐ × 6 ·····► ·····► 96

☐ × 6 → → 72
☐ × 6 ·····► ·····► 132
☐ × 6 → double → → 24
☐ × 6 ·····► ·····► 60
☐ × 6 → → 120
☐ × 6 ·····► ·····► 240

T Complete the sequences on the stepping stones.

12   24   60

72   108   132

S Complete the ×12 multiplication facts.

1 × 12 = ☐   2 × 12 = ☐   3 × 12 = ☐

4 × 12 = ☐   5 × 12 = ☐   6 × 12 = ☐

7 × 12 = ☐   8 × 12 = ☐   9 × 12 = ☐

10 × 12 = ☐   11 × 12 = ☐   12 × 12 = ☐

Describe the pattern in the multiples of 12 using these words: increases, even, digit, ones.

_____

_____

_____

D In the numbers from 1 to 100 there are 8 multiples of 12. List the multiples of 12 in the numbers from 100 to 200. Will there be as many multiples of 12 from 200 to 300? Explain why you think this is.

_____

_____

_____

Make 12s

 T Mo and Erin are playing Snap. Help them join pairs that have the same value.

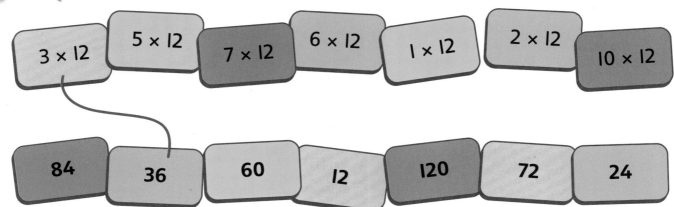

3×12 5×12 7×12 6×12 1×12 2×12 10×12

84 36 60 12 120 72 24

 S Write the missing numbers. Then make up some ×12 calculations.

$\boxed{} \times 12 = 60$ $7 \times 12 = \boxed{}$ $\boxed{} \times 12 = 48$

$\boxed{} \times 12 = 120$ $8 \times 12 = \boxed{}$ $11 \times 12 = \boxed{}$

$\boxed{} \times 12 = 36$ $\boxed{} \times 12 = 72$ $9 \times 12 = \boxed{}$

$\boxed{} \times 12 = \boxed{}$ $\boxed{} \times 12 = \boxed{}$

$\boxed{} \times 12 = \boxed{}$

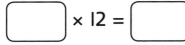

 D Calculate each answer and then write it as a ×12 multiplication.

$3 \times 16 = \boxed{} \times 12$ $6 \times 14 = \boxed{} \times 12$

$4 \times 18 = \boxed{} \times 12$ $3 \times 28 = \boxed{} \times 12$

$6 \times 18 = \boxed{} \times 12$ $4 \times 24 = \boxed{} \times 12$

$5 \times 24 = \boxed{} \times 12$ $8 \times 18 = \boxed{} \times 12$

Is it true that the answer to a multiplication stays the same if you multiply the first number and divide the second number by the same amount? Explain your answer.

Complete the calculations below using these numbers.

16   18   20   24   27   30   30   35   36   80

$2 \times 8 =$ [16] $5 \times 4 =$ [ ] $4 \times 6 =$ [ ]

$10 \times 3 =$ [ ] $3 \times 6 =$ [ ] $5 \times 7 =$ [ ]

$6 \times 5 =$ [ ] $8 \times 10 =$ [ ] $3 \times 9 =$ [ ]

One of the numbers has not been used. Write a multiplication with that answer. [ ] $\times$ [ ] $=$ [ ]

 Join pairs of calculations with the same product.

| 4 × 5 | 6 × 6 | 3 × 10 | 5 × 8 | 8 × 6 | 6 × 3 | 3 × 8 |

| 5 × 6 | 4 × 6 | 2 × 9 | 4 × 9 | 10 × 4 | 2 × 10 | 4 × 12 |

 Choose three numbers from the cloud to multiply together to make each target number.

2   6
3   4   5

[ ] $\times$ [ ] $\times$ [ ] $= 24$ [ ] $\times$ [ ] $\times$ [ ] $= 36$

[ ] $\times$ [ ] $\times$ [ ] $= 60$ [ ] $\times$ [ ] $\times$ [ ] $= 72$

[ ] $\times$ [ ] $\times$ [ ] $= 40$ [ ] $\times$ [ ] $\times$ [ ] $= 120$

Use the same set of numbers to make two more calculations with answers that are multiples of 12.

[ ] $\times$ [ ] $\times$ [ ] $=$ [ ]

[ ] $\times$ [ ] $\times$ [ ] $=$ [ ]

T Fill in the numbers on the bars and complete each calculation.

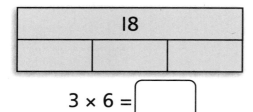

12		
4		

3 × 4 = [12]

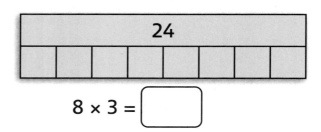

20			
5			

4 × 5 = [ ]

18		

3 × 6 = [ ]

24							

8 × 3 = [ ]

S Complete the calculations for each bar model.

35				
7	7	7	7	7

[ ] × [7] = [35]   [35] ÷ [7] = [ ]

56						
8	8	8	8	8	8	8

[ ] × [ ] = [ ]   [ ] ÷ [ ] = [ ]

36			
9	9	9	9

[ ] × [ ] = [ ]   [ ] ÷ [ ] = [ ]

D Write three different calculations that each bar model could represent. Include at least one division for each.

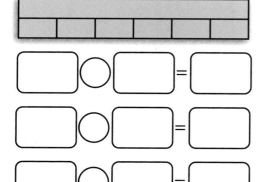

[ ] ◯ [ ] = [ ]

[ ] ◯ [ ] = [ ]

[ ] ◯ [ ] = [ ]

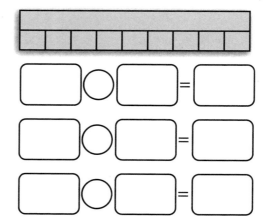

[ ] ◯ [ ] = [ ]

[ ] ◯ [ ] = [ ]

[ ] ◯ [ ] = [ ]

How many small squares are there in each larger square?

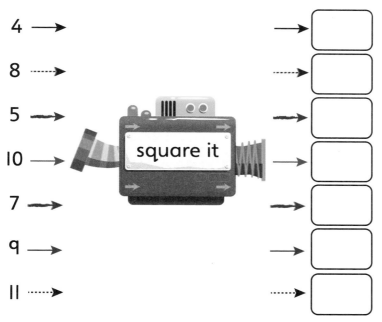

$1 \times 1 = \boxed{}$

$2 \times 2 = \boxed{}$

$3 \times 3 = \boxed{}$

$4 \times 4 = \boxed{}$

$5 \times 5 = \boxed{}$

$6 \times 6 = \boxed{}$

The number in the corner of each larger square tells you the number of smaller squares in each row and column.

 What numbers come out of the function machine?

$4 \longrightarrow$

$8 \dashrightarrow$

$5 \longrightarrow$

$10 \longrightarrow$ square it

$7 \longrightarrow$

$9 \longrightarrow$

$11 \dashrightarrow$

$\longrightarrow \boxed{}$

$\dashrightarrow \boxed{}$

$\longrightarrow \boxed{}$

$\longrightarrow \boxed{}$

$\longrightarrow \boxed{}$

$\longrightarrow \boxed{}$

$\dashrightarrow \boxed{}$

To square a number, you multiply it by itself.

 In each calculation a number is multiplied by itself to give the answer. Fill in all the missing numbers.

$\boxed{} \times \boxed{} = 25$

$\boxed{} \times 7 = \boxed{}$

$3 \times \boxed{} = \boxed{}$

$\boxed{} \times 9 = \boxed{}$

$\boxed{} \times \boxed{} = 144$

$\boxed{} \times \boxed{} = 16$

$8 \times \boxed{} = \boxed{}$

$\boxed{} \times 11 = \boxed{}$

$\boxed{} \times \boxed{} = 36$

Complete the multiplications. Multiply the number in the centre by the number in the next circle to find the outer number.

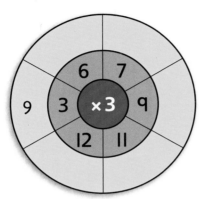 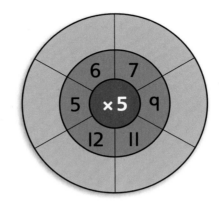 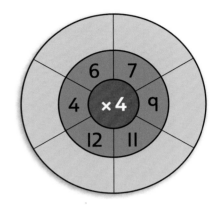

Complete the multiplications. Think about where to start each time to work out the number in the centre.

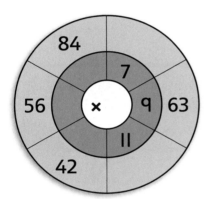 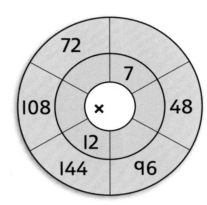 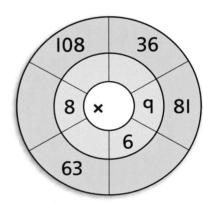

Fill in the grid. Use the numbers in the grid to work out the missing numbers.

Use your knowledge of times tables facts to find the missing numbers.

×			6	8				
6			48	54				18
	60		72			48		
11		77			132			
			56	63			77	
		54						27